STRANGER THAN FICTION:

WAR OF 1812

... with Parody Lyrics

STRANGER THAN FICTION:
WAR OF 1812

... *with Parody Lyrics*

by M. A. Noble

HOCKETT
Canton, NY

Stranger Than Fiction: War of 1812 is a work of humorous nonfiction. Any resemblance to historical persons is... *intentional.*

Copyright © 2015 M.A. Noble

All rights reserved

ISBN-10:0985834544
13:978-0-9858345-4-8

.

Acknowledgments

Thank you to Linda Batt for facilitating the original production and performance of *Stranger Than Fiction* with a grant funded by the New York State Council on the Arts through the St. Lawrence County Arts Council.

Thanks to Bob Garcia, Historian at Parks Canada, for information, review, and advice.

Thanks to E. Victoria Levitt, Bonnie Danis, Rosemary French, Patricia Reichhart, Leah Zelkowitz, Peggy Mooers, and the Canton Writers Group for review and suggestions.

CONTENTS

INTRODUCTION 1
   Are you as dumb as I was? 1
   Anchors Aweigh, Forward March 3
EMBARGO 4
   Parody: "O Grab Me!" 4
OVER THE OCEAN WAVES 6
   Parody: For Want of the Telegraph 7
IMPRESSMENT 9
   Parody: In the (Royal) Navy 10
EARTHQUAKES & NATIVES 11
   Parody: This Land 12
THE WAR HAWKS 13
   Parody: Payback Tango 13
(The STRANGENESS of it All) 16
PRIVATEERS 17
   Parody: Privateers We Be 19
CONDITIONS IN THE NORTH 22
   Parody: Battle of the Mosquito 22
DIVIDED STATES, SMUGGLING 24
   Parody: When You Pray With Papa 25

CONTENTS, continued

ST. LAWRENCE RIVER	27
Parody: The St. Lawrence River Runs Free	27
SPIES	29
Parody: Whistle Blowin' Mama	30
WOMEN IN CAMP	33
Parody: I Marry and I Tarry	33
LEADERS: Incompetent to Overconfident	36
Parody: Give Me Just a Little More Wine	37
TACTICS	39
Parody: The Ignoble Doom of York	40
Parody: Hello Dolly Madison	43
SURPRISING TWISTS	45
Parody: My Fleet's Bigger Than Yeo's	47
CANADA	49
Parody: NO Canada!	50
AT LAST	53
Non-Parody: Take Heart	54
NOTES	57
BIBLIOGRAPHY	61

STRANGER THAN FICTION:

WAR OF 1812

INTRODUCTION

Events of the War of 1812 surprised and fascinated me when I researched history for my first novel, *Taking Hart*. In fact, what I was reading seemed stranger than fiction. This odd war inspired me to write and perform twisted lyrics with such titles as "Whistle Blowin' Mama" (about whistle blower Laura Secord), and "Hello Dolly Madison" (British greeting to the first lady). The material was well received, and I agreed to record it in this irreverent guide—to give a few chuckles, yes, but also to challenge assumptions and make you think.

How can we make light of the war? After all, war was hell, then as now, with unspeakable suffering. But with time comes perspective and recognition of the ironies and foibles that accompany human conflicts, and laughing at our tragicomedy may be the only alternative to weeping for shame.

ARE YOU AS DUMB AS I WAS?

Let's get one thing straight: this is no comprehensive treatment of the War of 1812. It was a schizophrenic war fought in many locales, involving a variety of factions, interpreted and filtered through as many lenses. (In fact, the question of who won is still in debate!) No, this work highlights some of the interesting but lesser known quirks of a war that is little understood. And keep in mind, it is impossible to extract the "true story" of what happened when people of differing backgrounds, geography, and points of view offer a kaleidoscope of accounts. This book attempts to illustrate some ideas that may approach the truths of the causes, motives, and effects of the War of 1812.

Now be honest: What did you learn about the War of 1812 in school? That the British forced sailors off American ships to serve the Royal Navy? That the first lady saved a picture of George Washington before the British burned the White House? Maybe you even heard that Andrew Jackson beat the pants off the British in New Orleans. But did you know that the American national anthem was written on a British ship by an American attorney? A *lawyer*—and I find no evidence that he charged a dime for the work. What could be stranger than that?!

Did you know that British sailors were jumping ship to work on American vessels, for better working conditions? Or that U.S. slaves were "jumping ship" from the plantations to the British navy, where *they* found better conditions?[1]

In each section that follows, a topic is introduced and explored and then followed by lyrics. Many are notated with the name of a familiar song; please keep the tune in mind as you read the lyrics.

Warning: I pop quiz questions now and then (I know you miss school). Don't worry, they're easy.

First, let's set the stage—by setting sail.

ANCHORS AWEIGH and Forward March

In the early 1800s, Britain was busy fighting Napoleon and saw itself as a super hero for the world. The British needed all the sailors they could get, so they rounded up British-born men, even those found on American ships. They claimed that anyone born in Britain was a subject of the crown for life. But the British weren't always too picky about who they took off U.S. merchant ships. Sometimes they got American-born men as well, and they weren't afraid to treat them roughly. In addition, the British wanted to prevent trade with Europe, so they were stopping American ships to check their cargoes.[2]

By 1807, the U.S. was getting pretty darned mad: the British were stealing their citizens and blockading their coastline—after the U.S. had already won their war for independence. Who did the British think they were? They were not the boss of US!

EMBARGO

Thomas Jefferson decided to retaliate by stopping all trade with both Great Britain and France. The U.S. had supplied grain, meat, and other products; now the flow of goods would stop. The result? The embargo backfired. In fact, British officers in Canada were quite happy with Jefferson's embargo, because Canada picked up the slack in trade. They raised their glasses to *toast* Jefferson for helping to increase Canada's market![3]

Jefferson was mistaken in his assessment of foreign need for U.S. goods; he underestimated American dependence on overseas trade. The U.S. economy took a dive, and depression grabbed hold.[4]

If the War of 1812 were a musical, Uncle Sam would be singing his woes about the embargo—which spelled backwards, by the way, says, "O Grab Me!"

PARODY: (Embargo Backwards Spells) "O Grab Me!"

Tune: (author original)

> Jefferson thought he'd beat His Majesty
> But his embargo became a tragedy with
> Plummeting US economy
> The Brits could not care less while the US grew depressed
> And we learned embargo backwards spells O Grab Me!

O Grab Me, O Grab Me, O Grab Me!
O grab my trade, my sailors, and my dignity
O Grab Me, O Grab Me, O Grab Me!
Yes, the word embargo backwards spells O Grab Me.

QUIZ QUESTION: Short answer

What does "embargo" spell backwards?

(**O grab me** and take my pen away if you don't get this one!)

OVER THE OCEAN WAVES

While James Madison was president, U.S. anger was coming to a boil over the British orders of council, which had created the trade restrictions affecting the U.S. Having no interest in angering the U.S., the British were ready to talk about repealing the orders by May of 1812. But just before their meeting, the prime minister was assassinated by an angry businessman (over an unrelated matter).[5] Another month passed before the British got around to repealing the restrictions. *Won't the U.S. be pleased!* they surely thought.

But they couldn't email, text, or even telephone the President in the U.S.; in fact the good news took weeks sailing across the Atlantic. By the time the message arrived, a divided U.S. Senate had already voted 19-13 for war.[6]

What a shame. You'd think the British would at least have sent a telegram! Duh. In 1812 even the telegraph wouldn't be available for about thirty years (in plenty of time for the Civil War). But what if the telegraph *had* been available in 1812? Think of the things that might never have happened: the Northeast trying to break away from the Union, the smuggling between the U.S. and Canada, the naval battles on the Great Lakes and Champlain, the women noted for spying and fighting, the bungling and heroism that ruined and built careers, and the commanders written up as heroes...or goats.

PARODY: *For Want of the Telegraph*

Tune: (author original)

> The war of 1812, it was the strangest thing
> A lawyer wrote an anthem impossible to sing
> (They wanted) Freedom for the sailors, but the slaves? Nothin' doin'
> Whites escaped from British ships, with Blacks escaping to them
> *It happened for want of the telegraph*
> *The telegraph, the timely telegraph*
> Security was lax and the smuggling routes were hummin'
> A backward Paul Revere said "The Americans are comin'!"
> T'was hard to tell a friend from foe, that must be conceded
> The Northeast tried to break away, and almost seceded
>
> *It happened all for the want of the telegraph*
> *The telegraph, the timely telegraph*
> Macdonough sprung his ship around, his port guns to command
> On Erie Brits were fooled by Perry's "camel" on the sand
> Laura walked, and Dolly saved a picture from the wall
> Betsy was a hotshot with the fiery cannon ball
>
> *All for the want of the telegraph*
> *The telegraph, the timely telegraph*
> Landing parties unprepared with ladders far too short
> Troops were lacking focus, the missions they'd abort
> Americans used alcohol to cope and numb their chills

Canada said "grain's for food" —that's why they banned the stills

All for the want of the telegraph
The telegraph, the timely telegraph
The Brits repealed their orders, they sent a note one day
Hoping to avoid the war with their communique
Some say it was because the ship was too darned slow
That good ol' Jimmy Madison, he gave the war a "Go!"
It happened all for the want of the telegraph
A telegram might have saved twenty thousand
A telegram could've righted many wrongs
If the telegraph had been invented sooner
Then we might be singing a different song!

QUIZ QUESTION: Multiple choice

What communications device was invented between 1812 and the Civil War?

A. Smoke signals

B. The telephone

C. The printing press

D. The carrier pigeon

E. The telegraph

(Should I *wire* you the answer...or would you prefer **E** mail?)

IMPRESSMENT

Did you ever find that the solution to one problem only created a worse problem? The British problem was that they needed lots of sailors to fight Napoleon. When the Napoleonic Wars started, Britain had around 16,000 ships; just four years later, they had more than seven times as many, nearly 119,000. The British had only half as many sailors as they needed.[7] Compounding the problem were bad conditions on British ships, leading many British sailors to sign on to American merchant ships. The Royal Navy started plucking sailors off American ships, but they weren't very picky about who they took. They claimed that they were taking only British men, since they considered anyone born in Britain a subject of the king. But sometimes they got men born in America. Though the U.S. had fought and won the war for independence, Britain was not acknowledging U.S. sovereignty. Brutal British press gangs forced sailors off U.S. ships, and this impressment put a wrinkle in relations. The British solution to getting more sailors angered U.S. citizens and created negative PR. The bad public relations did nothing but help cause another war.[8]

Perhaps the British should have used a better marketing campaign to attract sailors—and impress upon them the benefits of serving The Royal Navy.

PARODY: In the (Royal) Navy

Tune: "In the Navy" by Jacques Morali, Henri Belolo, and Victor Willis

> Where the air is fresher, where you boys can measure
> Up to all you're meant to be
> With a purpose holy, we will beat Napole-an
> And set the whole world free
>
> In the Navy...You know that's where you belong
> Royal Navy...You're British subjects all along
> In the Navy...You think America's best
> Royal Navy...But on our ships you'll be impressed
>
> In the Navy, Royal navy, In the navy
> You must give your king his due
> Royal Navy...In a position just for you
> In the Navy! Come join the Royal Sails
> Royal Navy...Or meet the cat o' nine tails!
> In the Navy, His Majesty's Royal Navy!

QUIZ QUESTION: Multiple choice; complete the sentence.

American sailors who were impressed by the British...

A. admired the royal fleet.

B. were pressed to serve against their will.

C. volunteered to sail against Napolean.

(The press gangs forced the Americans onto British ships.)

EARTHQUAKES & NATIVES

What if you saw this news flash: *EARTHQUAKE, 8.8 on the Richter scale!* What geographical area would come to mind? Mexico? California, U.S.? Japan?

How about the American Midwest? Would you guess *Missouri*? Just before the war, from the end of 1811 through early 1812, a series of powerful earthquakes rocked the continent—centered far inland in what would become Missouri. It made the Mississippi river run backwards (at least part of it). The earth split open in many fissures, and the skies were smoggy and bad smelling. Tremors were felt in distant Washington, D.C. and Montreal. The quake caused church bells to ring as far away as Boston.[9]

Some native tribes thought the quake was an omen and that the Great Spirit was angry over the loss of native lands to the U.S. The Shawnee chief, Tecumseh, persuaded other tribes to join the British against the U.S.—another reason the Americans became angry enough to declare war.[10]

The U.S. wanted to expand westward into native territories, but the British were giving weapons to the natives and encouraging them to raid white settlements. Naturally, the new Americans were not happy.[11]

There were many players in the War of 1812—multiple factions of Americans, British, Canadians, and native tribes.

People still argue over who won. But almost everybody agrees on who lost. For helping their British ally, the Natives had been promised a territory of their own, but they got nothing in the end. In fact, the Native Americans ended up losing much of what they already had. They fought bravely and trusted the word of their ally, but the British broke their earlier promises during treaty negotiations.[12]

As a result, the natives were subjected to the "manifest destiny" of the U.S. Can you imagine what the natives' lament might sound like?

PARODY: *This Land*

Tune: "This Land is Your Land" by Woody Guthrie; "Don't Fence Me In" by Cole Porter (lyrics with Robert Fletcher)

> This land was in our hand, until you made demands
> And we lost out on Manhattan Island
> You clear our land of trees and push us to the seas
> But this land was made for roaming free
>
> Don't hem me in, take your saddle
> And skedaddle on back from where you came
> Leave us and go, even so we know
> The land will never be the same
> You call us savage when we protect our nations
> Hobble us and herd us onto reservations
> In the future you'll be facing litigation—don't hem me in.

THE WAR HAWKS

Many of the U.S. northerners were Federalists; they had no interest in a war that would harm their economy and come between friends, relatives, and trading partners along the nebulous northern border. But congress was populated with new southern Republicans, full of pride in America's status as a sovereign nation. They were eager to live up to the legacy of their fathers who had fought for independence.[13]

These southern men took issue with the way Britain was treating the U.S., and they got fired up about trade restrictions, impressment, native raids, and the burning of Washington. They wanted to punish the British. They were confident in their footwork. You might say they danced the Payback Tango.

PARODY: Payback Tango

Tune: "Cellblock Tango" (from the musical *Chicago*) by John Kander; lyrics by Fred Ebb

> (Spoken:)
> Scalpings, impressment, fire, raids!
> Scalpings, impressment, fire, raids!
>
> *We met them coming, we sent them running,*
> *We really cut them to the core.*
> *Who could ignore it? They're asking for it!*
> *You would have done the same and more.*

(Spoken:)
Our brave fathers fought hard for independence
We thought we'd kicked the bums out!
But they didn't get the message...
They messed with our commerce, stole our sailors,
Even armed the tribes to raid our settlements.
So we decided to take their Canada!

(Spoken:)
But they were confident...when we sailed into
York to seize their ships, they blew them up!
Thought they were pretty hot stuff.
And you know? They were right...
When we burned York to the ground.

We met them coming and sent them running,
We really cut them to the core.
Who could ignore it? They're asking for it!
You would have done the same and more.

(Spoken:)
They came and burned our capitol.
What's worse, they ate our food and drank our wine!
So they thought they'd have it easy,
Thought they'd have Baltimore for dessert...
But we put them on a diet.

(Spoken:)
Then they got a taste for creole,
Thought they'd devour New Orleans
But they learned the Big Easy really wasn't
With Jackson, sharpshooters, pirates, and free blacks
They lost their appetite
Must've got heartburn—when they...
Ate
Our
Lead.

We met them coming, we sent them running,
We really cut them to the core.
Who could ignore it? They're asking for it!
You would have done the same and more.

Quiz Question: T or F (True or False)

The northern Federalists were angry enough at the British to declare war.

(Southerners Clay and Calhoun would give you an **F** for missing this.)

The STRANGENESS of it All

It was an oddball war, with countless battles, extreme conditions, heroes and antiheroes, and all kinds of motives. Multiple parties were in conflict in various settings on land and water; there were divisions within parties that were supposed to be on the same side. There were so many unusual, even ludicrous, happenings that it's impossible to summarize the war. But let's take a look at just a few of the conditions and resulting acts of cleverness, incompetence, revenge, selfishness, and heroism.

PRIVATEERS

At the outbreak of war, the Americans had only sixteen ships in their navy. How could the U.S. hope to go up against the greatest naval power on earth, even if the British were fighting France at the same time?[14]

It was because the U.S. had a magic wand: they could conjure navy ships out of thin air. How's that, you ask? Here's the deal: they turned privately owned vessels into *privateers*.

If you were a private citizen who owned a ship, you could apply for a "Letter of Marque" from the government. If approved, you could be a privateer; you could raid enemy ships and divide up the profits. Of course you could not attack ships of your own country (or allies) or you'd be a *pirate*.

During the war, when there were only about twenty-some navy ships, there were more than five hundred privateers. The navy had fewer than six hundred guns (cannon), but the privateers added nearly three thousand. The navy captured about two-hundred-fifty ships compared to more than twelve hundred by the privateers, who captured about $40 million in prizes.[15]

Unconstrained by the rules of the navy, privateering men were clever and resourceful. The *Paul Jones* from New York City had just three guns when it met the British *Hassan*, with its fourteen. So the privateers painted some logs black and put them in the gun ports. The British were fooled into surrendering. In order to outrun the enemy, Thomas Boyle lightened one of his ships by throwing guns and spare sails overboard; his sailors sawed deck rails to give the guns more range. The ship *America* was so successful the British built a special frigate just to chase her down. They failed.[16]

(To be fair, the British had successful privateers of their own, many sailing out of Halifax, Nova Scotia. More than 700 U.S. merchant ships ended up as prizes there.)[17]

Many U.S. privateers operated off the mid-Atlantic coast, but there were also privateers on at least one inland river. The St. Lawrence was a critical waterway for the British sending supplies to Kingston in Upper Canada. Food, weapons, and even military pay were sent in flat-bottom boats called *bateaux*, protected only by a gunboat or two through a maze of channels and islands where enemies could hide.

In July 1813, a British convoy lost fifteen bateaux of pork and munitions to American privateers. The *Fox* and *Neptune* took those stolen boats up Cranberry Creek, east of Alexandria Bay, New York. The British sent a ship to block the entrance to Goose Bay, below the creek. They must have thought the Americans naïve: up the creek with no place to go. The British sent a smaller gunboat up the river to catch the privateers—but did they ever get a surprise. The Americans had gone onshore and sneaked downriver behind the gunboat, where they felled a tree across the water. Now the British gunners were up the creek with no retreat and were easily captured. The Americans floated the stolen supply boats past the British vessel by cutting through a swamp. (The men in Kingston must have stayed hungry—at least they never got *that* shipment of pork.)[18]

Without navy rules, a privateer's life was probably much like that of a pirate. We've all seen the romanticized version of a pirate's life portrayed by Hollywood...and what could be more romantic than the St. Lawrence River's 1000 Islands? Still, it couldn't have been too glamorous, privateering in gunboats in the north. You couldn't always use sails as you sneaked around the islands and shoals; you had to be ready to man the oars. It could be a cold, wet, and hungry life.

PARODY: Privateers We Be

Tune: "A Pirate's Life for Me" (Disney's Pirates of the Caribbean attractions) by George Bruns; lyrics by Xavier Atencio

> Row row, heave ho, a privateer I be
> We brace the yards for a river breeze
> Far inland from the seven seas
> We hide among the island trees
> Chin up me maties and row
> Row row heave ho, a privateer I be
>
> We push with poles, we pull the oars
> A sharp eye out for shallow shores

A privateer be never bored
Chin up me maties and row
Row row, heave ho, a privateer I be

We labor hard, we wait in the cold
Perchance to profit before we're old
We suffer and starve to find the gold
Chin up me maties and row
Row row, heave ho, a privateer I be

We strike the sails and out the sweeps
We hug the shore and silently creep
Upon the enemy fast asleep
Chin up me maties and hear
Row row heave ho I be a privateer

We'll take their ammo, pork and bread
Their soldier pay'll be ours instead
We'll find the loot or we'll soon be dead
Chin up me maties and cheer
Row row, heave ho, I be a privateer

But the lion's share goes to the boss
The crew divides the remaining dross
My paltry share won't cover my loss
And I face my gravest fears
Row row, heave ho, I be a privateer
Row row, heave ho...I shed my private tears.

Quiz Question: Multiple choice

If you were an American with a boat, you could attack a British ship if you had a _____

A. Telegram

B. Letter of Marque

C. Order of Council

D. Mark of Piracy

E. Skull & Bones

(You must **B**e very attentive to get high marques for this.)

CONDITIONS IN THE NORTH

Difficult terrain, miserable weather, and bad camp conditions plagued the north. Too little food and too much alcohol contributed to health issues that claimed thousands. So many men succumbed to starvation, colds, pneumonia, malaria, measles, pleurisy, dysentery, and typhoid fever that there was a constant drone of funeral music in camp. In fact, it got so demoralizing in at least one camp, the dirges were banned.[19]

People still argue over who won the war: some say the British, some say the Canadians, some say the U.S.—and some even claim the smugglers came out on top.

But I will tell you exactly who won. While the British, Americans, Canadians, and Natives fought in the woodland heat and in the cold and wet swamps of the northern river and lake areas, there emerged a clear winner: the mosquito. (And the black fly. And other pests.)

PARODY: Battle of the Mosquito

Tune: "Battle of New Orleans" by Jimmie Driftwood; "The Black Fly Song" by Wade Hemsworth

> We fired our muskets, the skeeters kept a comin'
> They flew formation, the numbers seem to grow
> Aerial squadrons zeroed in to get us
> We lost more blood to them than to the foe

Was early spring the regiment did go
To fight up north, Ontario
Hungry and tired but our hearts were stout
No enemy guns could have caused our rout

But the black fly, the little black beast
Strafing my front side, stickin' in my teeth
Chafing the back side ever out of reach
Way up Ontario-i-o-i-o, and down my breeches low

Flies & mosquitos everywhere I see
They suck my blood and they torment me
I try to aim but they grab my gun
It's not from the foe but the bugs I run!

And the black fly, the little black beast
Strafing my front side, stickin' in my teeth
Chafing the back side ever out of reach
Way up Ontario-i-o-i-o, and down my breeches low

Quiz Question: Multiple choice

There was a time when music was banned in the army camp. Why did they stop playing the music?

A. It gave away the position to the enemy
B. It distracted men from battle
C. It was depressing to hear death dirges

(Can you **C** the answer?)

DIVIDED STATES, SMUGGLING

Health issues were a big problem, but sometimes people were their own worst enemies. Those who voted for war did not understand their own countrymen. While the southern Republicans wanted war, northeasterners were against it because their economy depended on the trade with the so-called enemy. The northern Federalists even discussed seceding from the U.S. (The Confederate states of the Civil War were not the first to threaten to leave the union.)[20]

The young war hawks from the south did not understand the northern citizens who looked on Canadians—and even British—across the border as their friends and trading partners. On opposite banks of the St. Lawrence, they mirrored each other in looks and background, and it was hard to tell friend from foe. (The British across the border lived on smuggled American beef.)[21]

Up north, the U.S. eagle got along with the British lion. In fact, a sign just across the border spelled it out: "If you don't scratch, I won't bite."[22]

Many northerners were simple farmers and traders, struggling to make a life for their families. But among them were some powerful forces.

David Parish, from a prominent Scottish merchant family, operated out of Ogdensburg, New York. He made money on both sides of the border. He didn't want the war interfering with business, yet he loaned millions of dollars to the war effort.[23]

What!? Was he crazy? Crazy like a fox. Think of him as a lobbyist buying a promise from Madison to keep war away from *his* territory (even though his territory was probably the best place for the U.S. to cut off the British supply line). But maybe we should think of Parish as a pious and patriotic man: loyal to his religion of remuneration, a patriot of the cause of profitability—and leading his choir in a heavenly psalm.

PARODY: *When You Pray With Papa*

Tune: "When You're Good to Mama" (from the musical *Chicago*) by Queen Latifah and Taye Diggs

> The tenant farmers toil with rake and hoe
> But they'll tell you I'm the best at raising...dough
> I rub my fellows' backs and they rub mine
> We're patriots in a common cause...it's called the bottom line
>
> I say a little proverb each and every day:
> "If you put the plow in, you'll be making hay"
>
> The milk of human kindness is worth the living for
> What profits others by the pint I milk for gallons more

When you need assistance I'm glad to lend a hand
I slide it in your pocket and out comes fifty grand

Eagle scratches Lion, with talons sharp and long
I tickle Leo's back and let him scratch my itching palm

When southern troops come marching to stop our border trade
I grease Old Jimmy's hand to point the guns the other way

When beef runs low up north, I'm glad to take their shilling
When dollars beg for cannon balls, my foundry makes a killing

To live a life worthwhile, you must be devout
When the plate is passed 'round, there'll be plenty to take out
Be a friend to all men, give what they want most
Let them pick the carcass while you enjoy the roast

So what's the one conclusion we can bring this number to?
When you pray with Papa, Papa preys on you!

ST. LAWRENCE RIVER

People on both sides of the border used the same flowing highway to trade and visit and smuggle goods. Also, the British sent military supplies up the river as Americans sailed downriver in attempts to stop them.[24]

But make no mistake. The St. Lawrence was no doormat. This was long before the Seaway and its locks system made for a smooth journey. Depending on its whimsy, it could drop you in the rapids, it could strand you in the shallows, and it could betray you amongst its 1000 islands.

The St. Lawrence was a character with a head of its own. And if you listened carefully to its lapping waters, you could hear its gentle tongue-in-creek lullaby.

PARODY: The St. Lawrence River Runs Free

Tune: "St. Lawrence River" by Mitch Miller

> Row, row, row the river; row, row, yon and hither...but
> Master you'll never be; the St. Lawrence River runs free
>
> Northern or southern, I take no one's bossing
> I'm loyal to none, my shores are made for double crossing
> To some I'm supply-way,
> To others I am a smuggler's highway

The sultans of trade keep their own law and order
They'll pay a pretty sum to keep the war from their border
"The war's not for me," they say
"We're only trading naturally."

My south flank runs cattle, with a wink and a holler
I flow the straight and narrow, but I'll turn on a dollar
Don't count on me, I run either way to the sea

Row, row, row the river; row, row, yon and hither...but
Master you'll never be; the St. Lawrence River runs free
The St. Lawrence River runs free!

QUIZ QUESTION: Multiple choice

In the war of 1812, the St. Lawrence River was an important means of transportation; any of the following could delay passage on the St. Lawrence EXCEPT ___

(Which did *not* hold up progress on the river?)

A. waiting to enter the Eisenhower locks.

B. running aground on a shoal.

C. maneuvering around the rapids.

D. threading your way through the 1000 Islands.

(Having **A** good memory helps here. The Seaway, enabling navigation, was not created until the 1950s.)

SPIES

We've all heard of the resources of British spies: the skills, the daring...the secret weapons. Even in the War of 1812, the British in Canada knew the value of gathering intelligence. (Do you hear that James Bond theme music in the background?)

Okay, the name of the spy was not James—it was John. John Henry is sometimes called the spy who started the war of 1812. This British guy was hired by the governor general of Canada to gather information in the U.S. about divisions among the Americans and to encourage divisiveness. But the governor-general died and John Henry had trouble collecting his pay; he ended up selling questionable documents to President Madison and Secretary of State Monroe for $50,000. ($50K was nothing to sneeze at. Madison really could've used some new ships, maybe some supplies for the fighting men.) So here in the U.S., the government got a lot of flak from Federalists for wasting that $50,000.[25]

Back to the point: the British had their spies. But if you think a spy needed James Bond's skills in the War of 1812, think again. All he had to do was open the newspaper to read the details of U.S. troop movements. Heck, a person could walk right into the army camps and see for himself the condition of the troops. Or he could even buy information: there were citizens on both sides of the border who would sell out.[26]

But some citizens made great sacrifices, even taking on dangerous secret agent roles—like Laura Secord of the Niagara region in Upper Canada. How did she get involved? (No, she was not a chocolate supplier.)

The Americans planned to attack nearby Beaver Dams. The road was a mess. It took the American Major Chapin days of slogging through the mud with his troops and cannon. They stopped for rest and food at Queenston. At the Secords, where they were billeted, they didn't know the lady of house was listening to their plans...and making a plan of her own, to scurry through the woods ahead of them. The Americans ended up getting beaten. Laura Secord became famous for blowing the whistle on the Americans.[27]

A sadder and wiser Major Chapin probably would have sung something like this about Laura Secord, the whistle-blower.

PARODY: Whistle Blowin' Mama

Tune: "Pistol Packing Mama" by Al Dexter

> Chorus:
> *Lay that whistle down, Babe, lay that whistle down*
> *Whistle blowin' Mama, lay that whistle down*
>
> We spent two days hauling guns and cannon through the mud
> Stopped for food and raised a glass 'til we were feeling numb

The men and I got talking free, thought we were alone
Took no heed of the kitchen maid, plotting on her own

(*Chorus*)

Through brush and swamp and rough terrain
She scrambled in her gown
'Til the Iroquois at Beaver Creek
Passed on her warning sound
They laid a trap and sprang it
Before we raised a dust
That little lady'd turned our own
Ambush back on us

(*Chorus*)

The moral of the story is,
When stopping in a clearing
Make sure the lady of the house is far away
And hard of hearing
Better off to keep right on
Through mud and swamp and thistle
Than risk a strong willed woman
Hell bent to blow her whistle!

(*Chorus*)

QUIZ QUESTION: Short answer

Laura Secord is famous because she...

A. played a musical whistle.

B. warned the British of an American attack.

C. warned the Americans the British were coming.

D. served hot chocolate to the troops.

(The answer is a **B**rave action.)

WOMEN IN CAMP

Other women became involved in war battles—some risked their lives to carry information, like Laura Secord, and some took direct part in battle like Betsy Doyle, who loaded red-hot cannon shot at Ft. Niagara.[28]

But a number of women worked behind the scenes, living in army camps with their husbands. For every one hundred soldiers in camp, only six women were chosen by lottery to stay. Wives in camp did sewing, nursing, cooking, and cleaning. If her husband died, a camp woman had a grace period of three to six months to stay there, and then she had to leave—or marry someone else in camp. Some women married four or five times in as many months.[29]

It was a hard life for women who lost their husbands; they probably tried singing their cares away.

PARODY: I Marry and I Tarry

Tune: (author original)

> When I married John Travis I gave him my heart
> I said I would follow 'til death do us part
> I followed, and death did us part on the field
> My heart is still John's, but the balance is Neal's
>
> I marry and tarry and marry again
> I do what I can to survive

I marry and tarry and if that's a sin
I'll stop with number five

You went out one day and did never come back
I mourned as I could but the war gave no slack
I vowed to be true and I've kept up my word
In fact I've been true...to a second and third!

I marry and tarry, is that so bad?
We do what we can to survive
Is it better to offer your moral support
To only one man or to five?

Love is a luxury hard to come by
So soon after vows, in the dust they lie
I'm lucky to have bread or biscuit to eat
And find a man breathing and still on his feet

We marry and tarry and marry again
We do what we can to survive
We cook and we sew for the fighting men
Our aim is to keep us alive
To keep us all alive!

QUIZ QUESTION: Multiple Choice

The soldier's wife could live in the army camp...

A. when she was chosen by lottery

B. if her husband lived in camp

C. if she remarried a man in camp

D. A plus B and sometimes C

(Death was a constant worry for a soldier's wife.)

LEADERS: Incompetent to Overconfident

You've heard how Major Chapin made a major mistake allowing loose talk around a spy. He wasn't the only leader to make mistakes. There are numerous stories of lapses in judgment. Some leaders were too timid to make a stand, some too eager. With heavy attire and weaponry, one commander jumped out of a boat into too-deep water and nearly drowned. The U.S. commander at Lake Huron's Fort Mackinac in 1812 was not told the war was declared, and the fort was easily captured.[30]

Then there was the British colonel who made his troops remove their flints so the guns wouldn't go off prematurely and warn the enemy. As his men scaled the walls of the fort, they found that their ladders were too short: they could not return fire and were sitting ducks. (The siege of Fort Erie resulted in British carnage when a store of ammo exploded.)[31]

The U.S. had trouble finding experienced officers to fight the War of 1812. Many were old out-of-shape heroes from the Revolution, and many had big egos (some of them seemed more interested in dueling each other than in winning the war).[32]

One notorious leader was Major General James Wilkinson. Despite his history of pilfering, shady deals, and betrayal in the south, he was offered a post in the north. He was slow to travel and took advantage of every stop where he could feed his ego and his appetite. Meanwhile, troops in the north waited in the cold.[33]

They were cheered when Wilkinson arrived; his pretty speeches were inspiring. Trouble was, he was better at talking, eating, and drinking than acting. When he finally started the move to attack Montreal, he was slow and obvious. He lost badly at Crysler's Farm though he greatly outnumbered the enemy. But his words were his swords, and he always found a way to claim success from a failure—or blame someone else.[34]

PARODY: *Give Me Just a Little More Wine*
Tune: "Give Me Just A Little More Time" by Albert E. Brumley

> Chorus:
> *Give me just a little more time for war,*
> *Give me just a little more time*
> *So many ears to fill with cheers*
> *Many cups to fill with wine*
> *Gotta make some deals and take free meals*
> *Before I leave the town behind*
> *I'm ready when you call for war but*
> *Give me just a little more wine*

Well I'm ready every day to lead the way
to that city called Montreal
I hear a lot of doubt, they say time is runnin' out to shoot the rapids before the fall

Well I need a little time to set my line and lead the
battle from behind
I'm ready when you call for war, but
Give me just a little more wine.

(*Chorus*)

Need adjustment time for the northern clime or I'd
never even hesitate
I need a little time for medicinal wine and pain-
killers to acclimate
When we face a blow by a smaller foe and
chances are looking slim
I'm ready to call victory,
I'm Master of the Art of Spin

(He's ready to call victory, he's Master of the Art of Spin!)

QUIZ QUESTION: Multiple Choice

What was Wilkinson's weapon of choice?

A. musket

B. speech

C. song

D. fire

E. pistol

(This could have **B**een an oral exam.)

TACTICS

There was plenty of bungling on both sides in the War of 1812, but there were also some clever tactics. For example, the use of bugle calls.[35]

Suppose you're camping with a small force of regulars. From the woods to the west you hear the enemy's bugle call to advance.

You're frazzled! But you think: *Okay, maybe I can take them.* Then from the north you hear another bugle call, for pursuit.

And then from the northeast, you hear the call to *charge.*

The enemy must be greater than you thought! You change plans, do a hasty retreat to the south, maybe even surrender...

And you were just fooled by three buglers distributed to make you think the enemy outnumbered you.

TACTICS: BURNING I

It is important to keep your wits in a tense situation. But the troops facing hardship and failure sometimes let frustration impair their judgment. And when muskets and cannon (or bugles) failed to impress the enemy, they resorted to something with more fire power...the power of fire.

Americans and British started torching each other's forts and towns in retribution. Today's city of Toronto was the town of York in the early 1800s. The Americans decided to attack

York and take a British ship, though Kingston was likely the more valuable prize. (The Americans chose the target that offered more chance of victory; also, Kingston's harbor was blocked by ice.)[36]

In York, the British destroyed their ship rather than let it fall into American hands. They blew up their own fort, likely by accident, injuring many Americans and killing their leader. Then U.S. troops went crazy, looting and destroying things. They set a fire that made the Brits pretty hot under the collar.[37] (In Toronto, you might imagine you can still hear those crackling conflagrations today!)

PARODY: The Ignoble Doom of York

Tune: "The Noble Duke of York" (from traditional English nursery rhyme "The Grand Old Duke of York)

> They burned the town of York
> They had 4000 men
> They beat the foe but lost the ships
> They came to steal from them
> And when they lost their general
> They forgot the words he said
> To "protect the local properties"
> And looted them instead
>
> Chorus:
> *And when you're hot, you're hot*
> *And when you're not, you're not*

And when you're lit up for revenge,
The firing never stops

They burned the town of York
Not just the army store
The blazes made the Yorkers burn
To even up the score

(*Chorus*)

TACTICS: BURNING II

Revenge burnings went on back and forth after the Americans burned York. The British finally retaliated along the Atlantic coast when they went up the Chesapeake Bay and headed for Washington, D.C. They met the Americans in nearby Bladensburg.

The interesting thing about the American troops gathered to resist the British, aside from their blunders, was that they included several government officials—including the President of the United States! (Maybe *that's* why the Americans did so badly.) He was not evacuated by Marine One to a safe place, oh no. In 1813, government men took up arms. Bladensburg was the only U.S. battle where the President and the secretaries of war, navy, and state were present. As the battle proceeded, conflicting orders and failure to communicate created chaos.[38]

The Americans were ineffective against the British. In fact, more British were killed by nature than by the defenders.[39] It was August, and some soldiers succumbed to heat stroke; others were whipped by a freak tornado.[40]

President Madison was pretty impressed by what he saw on the battlefield. He had been opposed to the U.S. having a standing military—but after comparing the performance of a trained army to that of the called-up militia, he changed his mind. Probably realizing that untrained soldiers did more harm than good, he came to appreciate the value of a well-trained standing military, which the U.S. has had ever since.[41]

After the battle at Bladensburg, the Americans ran away and the British headed for Washington. Madison had sent notice to Dolly to get out of town. (He probably wished he could return to hearth and home, where the table was set, and food and wine were prepared for a dinner party. But it wasn't to be—at least not with the guests he'd planned.)[42]

Back at the White House, Dolly had used a spy glass off and on all day, watching for hubby James to return. Now she knew the British were coming, but she wouldn't leave, not her! Not even after the guards left. There she remained, intent upon stuffing documents into a carriage (and carriages were scarce, with all the citizens scrambling to get out of town).[43]

Supposedly, Dolly waited for George Washington's portrait, but it was taking too long to get it unscrewed from the frame so she had the frame broken and the canvas rolled up. Then she got the heck out of town before the British came, ate, and torched the building.[44]

What if there had been just a couple extra documents, a couple extra twists needed to roll the picture? If Dolly had not gotten away before the British arrived, how would they have greeted Mrs. Madison? Some think they might have taken her prisoner.

But maybe they would have been mollified by her Martha Stewart skills.

PARODY: Hello Dolly Madison

Tune: "Hello, Dolly!" by Jerry Herman; "Ring of Fire" by June Carter (Cash) and Merle Kilgore

> Hello Dolly, come back down from your folly
> George's picture cannot save you from our wrath
> Go find Jim and leave DC
> Our troops are more prepared than he
> You're smarter than your hubby, do the math!

> We see you've set the table, as a hostess you are able
> Your hospitality we would not spurn
> Cherry flambé's not on your menu
> But as guests the least we can do
> Is eat the blazing meal before it burns.

The house will burn, burn, turn to walls of white no longer
You will learn, learn, learn that our fire power's stronger

You're the brave one, they'll adore you
Even soldiers fled before you
Have no trepidation while we chill
There's no point in burning dinner
Since the war has made us thinner
We will torch the house when we have had our fill

The house will burn, burn, turn to walls of white no longer
You will learn, learn, learn that our fire power's stronger
Hello Dolly... and goodbye!

QUIZ QUESTION: Multiple Choice

Why did the British burn the white house?

A. They mistook it for Washington monument.

B. It was payback for the burning of York.

C. It was payback for the battle at Baltimore.

D. They overcooked Dolly's cherry pie.

(The answer should **B**e obvious. **A** monument hadn't been built yet. **C**ombat in that other city up the Chesapeake happened later. On the other hand, we can't be sure they didn't burn **D**olly's pie!)

SURPRISING TWISTS

The British torched Washington but, strangely enough, the fires were put out by a downpour. Along with a freak tornado, Mother Nature sent torrential rains that helped save Washington from being burned to the ground.

Otherwise, the British met little resistance in Washington and continued to Baltimore. Their Commander Ross must have felt pretty cocky as he rode into Baltimore, but that feeling would have been extinguished as he was shot right off his horse by riflemen—a bad omen for the British. In Baltimore, a well-coordinated U.S. force turned the tables on the greatest navy on earth.[45]

There were other surprising wins, due to planning, cleverness, and luck.

On Lake Champlain, Macdonough spring-loaded his anchor cables so that when his starboard guns were damaged he could spin the ship to aim his portside cannon at the enemy. He drove the British back to Canada.[46]

Did you know that on Lake Erie a *camel* enabled Commodore Perry to meet the enemy and capture the fleet? Perry's ship was stuck behind a sandbar. A camel was a device that could provide lift, using buoyancy boxes filled with water and fastened to the sides of the ship. Removing the water from the camel raised the ship so it could be moved out onto the lake.⁴⁷

In Oswego, a false tent camp was erected in the village to fool the British, who attacked the opposite fort instead.⁴⁸

But it was Lake Ontario where the great Arms Race took place, between U.S. and British Commodores Chauncey and Yeo. Loads of money was spent on vessels that would never see battle as the two commodores competed to build ships of greater size and power. Rather than engage in battle, they often maneuvered their ships around each other.⁴⁹

When the Americans were building the great ship *Superior* at Sackets Harbor, British Commodore Yeo set a blockade to prevent the completion of this ship, which would have given the Americans naval superiority. Even so, the Americans were able to sneak some of the new ship's armaments past the enemy. However, they could not bring in a huge cable, a big rope of hemp to be used for anchor or rigging. It was massive: nearly five tons. No way could they sneak that by Yeo's blockade. At least not by water. So what did the Americans do? They made a human chain of a hundred or more men and boys who carried the cable twenty miles over land from Sandy Creek! The carriers suffered a lot of bruising on their shoulders though they were padded with straw. When they arrived at Sackets Harbor, they were received with cheers, music, and a barrel of whiskey.⁵⁰

PARODY: *My Fleet's Bigger Than Yeo's*

Tunes: "My Dog's Better Than Your Dog" by Tom Paxton

    Chauncey thinks it chancy and Yeo's afraid to go
    Sail and risk their pretty ships to the cannon of the foe
    Instead they play at stacking decks and call across the bay
    In this big boys' competition here is what they say:

My fleet's bigger than your fleet
My fleet's bigger than yours
My fleet's better, it's got more fire power
My fleet's bigger than yours

    Chauncey built the finest ship but needed more supplies
    Yeo set out a blockade so that ship would never rise
    They snuck rigging and the guns in boats as they were able
    But Yeo caught on before they sailed that five-ton cable
    (Spoken:) They'd need a human ship to carry that

    The cable made its run o'er two hundred shoulders slung
    Two hundred yards moved on four hundred feet
    It rippled like a snake along the earth—not on the lake
    It was the newest member of the fleet

    (Spoken): And Chauncey said:
My fleet's bigger than your fleet
My fleet's bigger than Yeo's
My fleet covers both land and sea
My fleet's bigger than Yeo's.

STRANGER THAN FICTION

QUIZ QUESTION: Multiple Choice

Why did the people carry a big rope on their shoulders?

A. It would swell if it touched wet ground.

B. Shipping was far too expensive.

C. There was no UPS service in those days.

D. They wanted to avoid Yeo's forces.

(You should have no problem **D**eclaring the best answer. However, one could **C** how others might **B** argued as true.)

CANADA

Canada was not the country we know today. In the early 1800s, it was a group of colonies known as British North America. The "Canadas" were several British colonies, the two major ones being Ontario and Quebec.

Ontario was Upper Canada, and Quebec was Lower Canada (contrary to our thinking of north as up and south as down). The St. Lawrence River flows north, from the higher land near the Great Lakes to the lower lands of Quebec, and then to the ocean. Upper Canada was mostly British, Lower Canada mostly French. There wasn't much unity in the Canadas, between the colonies or even within one. Upper Canada was a patchwork of residents with various backgrounds and motives. Many had no interest in fighting a war.[51]

The U.S. thought they could punish the British by taking their North American possession. Thomas Jefferson had said taking Canada would be simply a matter of "marching." Neither he nor Madison realized that the residents were not eager to be liberated from the British, or that British Major General Brock's forces were well prepared for them (or that the ineptitude of some of their own American leaders would ensure failure).

Though the Canadas were smatterings of individuals, the War of 1812 itself helped build a sense of identity that would later forge the British colonies into a new nation.[52]

What if their identity had not been burnished by the War of 1812? What if we could travel back in time and alter something (maybe invent the telegraph!) so there had been no war of 1812? Would there be no Canadian national anthem? Would there be *NO Canada?*

PARODY: NO Canada!

Tunes: First and last lines of music: "O Canada!" by Calixa Levallée (English lyrics by Justice Robert Stanley Weir); additional music is author original.

> No Canada...
>
> Chorus:
> *No one oot and aboot eating fries with poutine;*
> *No hockey pucks to dodge or duck,*
> *And the red maple leaves flutter only on trees in the*
> *Autumn breeze*
>
> No Canada Goose cutting loose would have to (em)migrate
> No border patrol, no need to show your passport at the gate
> No loonies for all those curds and fries
> No toonies to drink that Canada Dry
> If northerners had lived a different fate

(Chorus)

No health care to cover when the black flies hover
And take you down
No Canadian ale warms your frozen tail when
You're landing on the ground
No red-suited mounty on a horse
No parliament on the hill, of course
If Canada were nowhere to be found

Would the maple sap even keep on runnin'
With Dion, Twain, and Lightfoot hummin'
Would we retire the vowels *oo* and *eh*?
We'll never know 'cause Canada is here to stay
Canada is here to stay

QUIZ QUESTION: Multiple Choice

The province of Ontario used to be called Upper Canada because...

A. it was upriver from Lower Canada.

B. it was settled by the upper crust.

C. it was near the ocean.

D. Mexico was then Lower Canada.

(The Atlas holds the clue.)

WAR OF 1812

AT LAST...

The war of 1812 was a small chunk of history with interesting moments. The military on either side were sometimes unfocused and ineffective, but there were remarkable moments of heroism, ingenuity, and leadership.

The final battle was in New Orleans. Andrew Jackson rounded up and crash-trained some frontiersmen, militia, blacks, and even pirates to repel the British. When the British attacked, they lost 2000 men—more than twenty times Jackson's loss of less than a hundred.[53] But it happened in January 1815 after the peace treaty was hammered out in Europe (remember, letters travelled slowly by ship, by carriage, or on foot.)[54]

Some said the battle of New Orleans was a wasted effort. Some historians say it injected the Americans with enthusiasm and unity. Though the treaty left conditions near status quo, the war gave the U.S. a respected place among nations.[55]

Here you've read only a sampling of events in the two-and-a-half-year war. But I hope you have enjoyed a different way of looking at the conflict, perhaps even learned something. Maybe that assumptions, shortcuts, and failure to assess critically can lead to unnecessary losses. Let's hope that someday we humans will learn to get along with each other better than we have in the past.

NON-PARODY: Take Heart

Tune: (Original)

    Take heart that life is not a game of chances
    Spread hope instead of clubs and cannonades
    Remember all of us are diamonds in the rough
    The hand you deal comes back to you in spades

    Take heart in the art of kindness
    Take heart when you only see defeat
    Take heart, have faith in the human race
    There's good inside of everyone you meet

END

Thanks for Reading!

Stranger than Fiction: War of 1812 was a fun and enlightening project to create and perform, and I hope you enjoyed the written version. If so, please let others know by leaving a review at Amazon.com.

Also, I am open to your feedback and ideas at the following address:

MANoble@rocketmail.com

ABOUT THE AUTHOR

M. A. Noble lives in St. Lawrence County in New York State between the Adirondack Mountains and the Canadian border along the St. Lawrence Seaway. Her past life included writing/editing for educational publishers. Now she loves to surf (far away), wakeboard (nearby), rock out on the drums (at home), and read or write (anywhere).

NOTES

[1] Alan Taylor, *The Civil War of 1812*, 104, 112-113, 327

[2] Ibid, 102-105

[3] Ibid 116, 119

[4] Ibid, 117. ; RandomHistory.com, "52 Interesting Facts," http://facts.randomhistory.com/war-of-1812-facts.html

[5] Barrell, Review of "Why Spencer Perceval Had to Die" by Andro Linklater, http://www.theguardian.com/books/2012/may/11/why-spencer-perceval-andro-linklater-review

[6] Toll, "Six Frigates," 329

[7] Taylor, *Civil War*, 103

[8] Ibid, 4

[9] City of New Madrid, "Strange Happenings," *New Madrid Missouri*, www.new-madrid-mo.us/index.aspx?nid=132

[10] Wei, "Red Stick Creeks," http://www.historiaobscura.com/category/uncategorized/native-american-history/

[11] *Encyclpedia of the Wars*, edited by Spencer C. Tucker, 57.

[12] Taylor, *Civil War*, 414-418, 426

[13] Ibid, 128

[14] Black, "A British View," *Naval History Magazine*, http://www.usni.org/magazines/navalhistory/2008-08/british-view-naval-war-1812

[15] American Merchant Marine at War, "American Merchant Marine and Privateers" *American Merchant Marine*, www.usmm.org/warof1812.html

[16] Ibid

[17] Garcia, Email message to author, Oct. 15, 2015.

57

[18] Snow, ed., "Bloody Battle," *Thousand Islands Sun*, http://www.rootsweb.ancestry.com/~nycalexa/hiscran.htm ; Fulton and Carpenter, "The Battle of Cranberry Creek" Pamphlet

[19] Taylor, *Civil War*, 287

[20] ConnecticutHistory.org, "The Hartford Convention--" *Hartford*, http://connecticuthistory.org/the-hartford-convention-today-in-history/

[21] Taylor, *Civil War*, 290-291

[22] Ibid, 271

[23] Ibid, 269-70

[24] WNED-TV Buffalo/Toronto, "St. Lawrence/Champlain Theater," *War of 1812*, http://www.pbs.org/wned/war-of-1812/historic-sites/st-lawrencechamplain-theater/

[25] Taylor, *Civil War*, 130-31

[26] Ibid, 336, 340-41

[27] Ibid , 225

[28] "Autumn 1812: Betsy Doyle" *National Park Service*, http://www.nps.gov/articles/betsy-doyle.htm

[29] "History of American Women Nurses," *History of American Women*, http://www.womenhistoryblog.com/2014/07/first-women-nurses.html; Wanchisn, "Transcript of Impact of the Women" *Impact of Women on the War of 1812*, https://prezi.com/sohzws0hpe8q/impact-of-the-women-on-the-war-of-1812/

[30] Taylor, *Civil War*, 153, 387

[31] Ibid, 397

[32] Ibid, 96-7, 324

[33] Ibid, 280-82

[34] Ibid, 279, 283, 285, 289

[35] Middle Horn Leader, "Evolution of the Bugle," *The Middle Horn Leader,* http://www.middlehornleader.com/Evolution%20of%20the%20Bugle%20--%20Section%202.htm

[36] Malcomson and Malcomson, "War of 1812: Battle" *HistoryNet* Historynet.com/war-of-1812-battle-of-york.htm ;
Taylor, *Civil War,* 214;
Garcia, email to the author.

[37] Taylor, *Civil War,* 214-217

[38] Maryland-National Capital Park and Planning Commission, "The Battle of Bladensburg," *Prince George County Department of Parks and Recreation,* http://www.pgparks.com/War_of_1812/History/The_Battle_of_Bladensburg.htm;
A&E Television Networks, "1814 British Capture," *History,* http://www.history.com/this-day-in-history/british-capture-and-burn-washington

[39] RandomHistory.com, "52 Interesting Facts." *Random Facts,* http://facts.randomhistory.com/war-of-1812-facts.html

[40] Maryland-National Capital Park and Planning Commission, *Your Passport,* Dept. of Parks and Rec, Prince George Co. MD, http://issuu.com/pgparks/docs/war_of_1812_brochure_v6;
Rainier Chapter National Society Daughters of the American Revolution, *War of 1812 The Second Revolution:* 18,
https://books.google.com/books?id=xM_AAwAAQBAJ&pg=PA18&lpg=PA18&dq=heat+stroke+war+of+1812&source=bl&ots=Ateb4VAGjH&sig=k3b7zS0-_Z82IXXc25Y_QITQ4l4&hl=en&sa=X&ved=0CCsQ6AEwAmoVChMI3dTyoM7wyAIVAVImCh29PgHF#v=onepage&q=heat%20stroke%20war%20of%201812&f=false
MilitaryHistoryNow.com, "The Tornado that Saved America," *MHN Military History Now,* http://militaryhistorynow.com/2013/05/22/rescued-by-a-tornado-the-1814-twister-that-saved-washington/

[41] Greenspan, "The British Burn Washington," *History in the Headlines,* http://www.history.com/news/the-british-burn-washington-d-c-200-years-ago

[42] Ibid

[43] Allgor, "A Perfect Union," *Truly Amazing Women Who are Changing the World*, http://trulyamazingwomen.com/the-women/dolley-madison-americas-first-lady

[44] A&E Television Networks, "Dolley Madison Saves Portrait," *This Day in History, History*, http://www.history.com/this-day-in-history/dolley-madison-saves-portrait-from-british ; Allgor, "A Perfect Union," *Truly Amazing Women Who are Changing the World*, http://trulyamazingwomen.com/the-women/dolley-madison-americas-first-lady

[45] Cowart, "The Shelling of Ft. McHenry," *John Cowart*, http://www.cowart.info/Americana/Star%20Spangled%20Banner/Star%20Spangled%20Banner.htm

[46] NHHC, "Unsung Heroes" *Naval History*, http://www.navalhistory.org/2010/09/11/unsung-heroes-of-the-battle-of-lake-champlain-2

[47] Howard, "War of 1812: Battle," *History Net*, http://www.historynet.com/war-of-1812-battle-of-lake-erie-oliver-perrys-miraculous-victory.htm

[48] Sturgill, "The Hero of Oswego," *Cecil Whig*, http://www.cecildaily.com/our_cecil/article_8f64f794-9f51-11e2-98ab-001a4bcf887a.html

[49] Taylor, *Civil War*, 233, 240

[50] Bettinger, "An Analysis of the Events," *USGenNet*, http://www.usgennet.org/usa/ny/county/jefferson/hounsfield/bettingerpaper.html

[51] Taylor, *Civil War*, 63

[52] Ibid, 444, 458

[53] A&E Television Networks, "Battle of New Orleans," *History*, http://www.history.com/topics/battle-of-new-orleans

[54] Taylor, *Civil War*, 418-19

[55] Ibid, 421

BIBLIOGRAPHY

A&E Television Networks, "1814 British Capture and Burn Washington." *History: August 24 This Day In History.* http://www.history.com/this-day-in-history/british-capture-and-burn-washington

A&E Television Networks, "Battle of New Orleans." *History.* http://www.history.com/topics/battle-of-new-orleans

A&E Television Networks, "British Prime Minister Assassinated." *This Day in History.* www.history.com/this-day-in-history/british-prime-minister-assassinated

A&E Television Networks, "Dolly Madison Saves Portrait from British." *This Day in History, History.* http://www.history.com/this-day-in-history/dolley-madison-saves-portrait-from-british

Allgor, Catherine. "A Perfect Union: Dolly Madison and the Creation of the American Nation" (excerpt). *Truly Amazing Women Who are Changing the World.* http://trulyamazingwomen.com/the-women/dolley-madison-americas-first-lady

American Merchant Marine at War, "American Merchant Marine and Privateers in War of 1812." *American Merchant Marine.* May 24, 2015. www.usmm.org/warof1812.html

Barrell, John. Review of "Why Spencer Percival Had to Die. by Andro Linklater. *The Guardian,* May 11, 2012. http://www.theguardian.com/books/2012/may/11/why-spencer-perceval-andro-linklater-review

Berton, Pierre. *Flames Across the Border.* Boston: Little, Brown and Company, 1981.

Bettinger, Blaine. "An Analysis of the Events Surrounding the Battle of Big Sandy and the Carrying of the Great Rope in 1814 and the Ensuing 185 years." *USGenNet,* Fall 1998/Spring 1999. http://www.usgennet.org/usa/ny/county/jefferson/hounsfield/bettingerpaper.html

Black, Jeremy. "A British View of the Naval War of 1812," *Naval History Magazine*. *US Naval Institute*, August 2008 (Vol. 22 No. 4). http://www.usni.org/magazines/navalhistory/2008-08/british-view-naval-war-1812

City of New Madrid, "Strange Happenings During the Earthquakes." *New Madrid Missouri*, 2005-2015. http://new-madrid.mo.us/index.aspx?nid=132

Concord Learning Systems, "The War of 1812, A Curious War" *Golden Nuggets of U.S. History*. http://laughtergenealogy.com/bin/history/war1812.html

ConnecticutHistory.org, "The Hartford Convention--Today in History: December 15," *Hartford*, http://connecticuthistory.org/the-hartford-convention-today-in-history/

Cowart, John W. "The Shelling of Ft. McHenry." *John Cowart's Web Page*, 2005. http://www.cowart.info/Americana/Star%20Spangled%20Banner/Star%20Spangled%20Banner.htm

Dudley, William S. Review of *How the British won the War: The Royal Navy's Blockades of the United States, 1812-1815* by Brian Arthur. *Reviews in History*. http://www.history.ac.uk/reviews/review/1215

Emerson Kent, "War of 1812 Timeline: 1812." *History for the Relaxed Historian*. http://www.emersonkent.com/history/timelines/war_of_1812_year_1812.htm

Encyclopedia of the Wars of the Early American Republic, 1783-1812, edited by Spencer C. Tucker. (Santa Barbara, Denver, Oxford, ABC-CLIO, 2014): 57.

Fulton, Roger and Michael Carpenter. "The Battle of Cranberry Creek in the War of 182: Fought Near Alexandria Bay, NY, July 1813." Pamphlet: Roger Fulton, Alexandria Bay, NY, 2005.

Garcia, Bob (historian, of Parks Canada). Email message to author, October 15, 2015.

Greenspan, Jesse. "The British Burn Washington, D.C., 200 Years Ago." *History in the Headlines, History,* Aug. 22, 2014. http://www.history.com/news/the-british-burn-washington-d-c-200-years-ago

Hickman, Kennedy. "War of 1812: Causes of Conflict." *About Education.* http://militaryhistory.about.com/od/warof1812/a/war-of-1812-causes_2.htm

Howard, E. "War of 1812: Battle of Lake Erie: Oliver Perry's Miraculous Victory." *History Net,* June 12, 2006. http://www.historynet.com/war-of-1812-battle-of-lake-erie-oliver-perrys-miraculous-victory.htm

Malcomson, Robert and Thomas Malcomson. "War of 1812: Battle of York." *History Net.* http://www.historynet.com/war-of-1812-battle-of-york.htm

Maryland-National Capital Park and Planning Commission, "The Battle of Bladensburg." *Prince George County Department of Parks and Recreation.* http://www.pgparks.com/War_of_1812/History/The_Battle_of_Bladensburg.htm

Maryland-National Capital Park and Planning Commission, "Your Passport to the War of 1812." *Department of Parks and Recreation, Prince George County MD.* Page: The Battle of Bladensburg http://issuu.com/pgparks/docs/war_of_1812_brochure_v6

Middle Horn Leader, "Evolution of the Bugle" (subtopic: The War of 1812). *Middle Horn Bugle.* http://www.middlehornleader.com/Evolution%20of%20the%20Bugle%20--%20Section%202.htm

MilitaryHistoryNow.com, "The Tornado that Saved America." *MHN Military History Now,* May 22, 2013. (The Storm that Changed History?). http://militaryhistorynow.com/2013/05/22/rescued-by-a-tornado-the-1814-twister-that-saved-washington/

Murano, Grace. "7 Strangest Wars." *Oddee.* March 19, 2009. http://www.oddee.com/item_96610.aspx

National Park Service U.S. Department of the Interior, "Autumn 1812: Betsy Doyle Helps Operate a Cannon to Defend Ft. Niagara." *National Park Service,* Nov 11, 2015. http://www.nps.gov/articles/betsy-doyle.htm

NHHC. "Unsung Heroes of Lake Champlain." *Naval History Blog,* Sept. 11, 2010. http://www.navalhistory.org/2010/09/11/unsung-heroes-of-the-battle-of-lake-champlain-2

North Carolina Military Project, "Little Known Facts of the War of 1812." *North Carolina in the War of 1812,* Sept. 4, 2009. http://nc1812.lostsoulsgenealogy.com/facts.htm

RandomHistory.com, "52 Interesting Facts About the War of 1812." *Random Facts* (Fact 24), http://facts.randomhistory.com/war-of-1812-facts.html

Snow, Jeanne, ed. "Bloody Battle of Cranberry Creek." *Thousand Islands Sun.* July 22, 1976 (after article by R. Gareth). http://www.rootsweb.ancestry.com/~nycalexa/hiscran.htm

Sturgill, Erika L. Quesenbery. "The Hero of Oswego NY: Elkton's Dr. George E. Mitchell." *Cecil Whig.* http://www.cecildaily.com/our_cecil/article_8f64f794-9f51-11e2-98ab-001a4bcf887a.html

Taylor, Alan. *The Civil War of 1812.* New York: Vintage Books, 2010.

Toll, Ian W. "Six Frigates: The Epic History of the Founding of the U.S. Navy." *Google Books,* 329 https://books.google.com/books?id=q9xfGcwEEqMC&pg=PA329&lpg=PA329&dq=war+of+1812+orders+of+council+prime+minister+assassin&source=bl&ots=IqkLJifQ5W&sig=FGXHTOLjoFb29mbfpAAzegVM3QA&hl=en&sa=X&ved=0CE4Q6AEwB2oVChMIjcf55OrOyAIVSsxjCh18Xgso#v=onepage&q=war%20of%201812%20orders%20of%20council%20prime%20minister%20assassin&f=false

Wanchisn, Danny. "Impact of the Women on the War of 1812." *Impact of Women on the War of 1812,* Kathleen Kosmowski, Feb 12, 2014. https://prezi.com/sohzws0hpe8q/impact-of-the-women-on-the-war-of-1812/

Wei, Jerilee. "The Red Stick Creeks and the Great Earthquakes of 1811-1812." *Historia Obscura,* July 16, 2014. http://www.historiaobscura.com/category/uncategorized/native-american-history/

Williams, T. Harry. *The History of American Wars.* New York: Alfred A. Knopf, 1981.

Wills, Garry. *James Madison.* New York: Henry Holt and Company, 2002.

WNED-TV Buffalo/Toronto, "Military Medicine in the War of 1812." *PBS The War of 1812.* http://www.pbs.org/wned/war-of-1812/essays/military-medicine/

WNED-TV Buffalo/Toronto, "St. Lawrence/Champlain Theater." *War of 1812,* Public Broadcasting Station. http://www.pbs.org/wned/war-of-1812/historic-sites/st-lawrencechamplain-theater/

www.ingramcontent.com/pod-product-compliance
Lightning Source LLC
Chambersburg PA
CBHW031419040426
42444CB00005B/640